PLAY BETTER GOLF
SHOTS FOR LOWER SCORING
How to play the trickier shots

Beverly Lewis

Illustrations by Ken Lewis

TIGER BOOKS INTERNATIONAL
LONDON

3152
This edition published in 1992 by
Tiger Books International PLC, London
© 1991 Colour Library Books Ltd, Godalming, Surrey
Printed and bound in Singapore
All rights reserved
ISBN 1-85501-225-1

Contents

Beverly and Ken Lewis

Beverly Lewis became a professional golfer in 1978 and has twice
been Chairman of the Women's Professional Golf Association. A PGA
qualified professional since 1982, she has played in many major
tournaments and is an experienced teacher. She has been a regular
contributor to *Golf World* magazine in the United Kingdom for six
years and is the only woman on their teaching panel. She has won
two tournaments on the WPGA circuit but now concentrates on her
teaching commitments.

Beverly is co-author of *Improve Your Golf* (published in the UK by
Collins Willow, revised edition), and has written the other titles in the
Golf Clinic Series. Her interests include music and playing the organ.

Ken Lewis trained at the Southend College of Art and then worked as
a commercial artist. He has illustrated many golf books, working with
players such as Peter Alliss, Alex Hay and Sandy Lyle. His projects
include illustrating newspaper instructional features and strips by
Greg Norman and Nick Faldo, and he works for *Golf* Magazine in the
United States. His hobbies include building and flying his own
aeroplane.

Introduction

When you were taught to hit a golf ball, you did so from a good lie, on flat, level ground, with no obstacles between you and your target. The irony of this is that, apart from the tee shots, you seldom get a shot played under these conditions. The ground can slope in any direction, which in itself can produce a curve to the ball's flight and if unanticipated can get you into trouble. So the first twelve chapters of this book explain in detail how best to play shots from uphill, downhill and sidehill lies, on the fairway, around the green and in bunkers. Your local course may be very flat and thus when you visit hillier courses, you are unprepared for the different stances and lies that you are bound to experience there.

The beginner's best friends should be the fairway woods, since these are versatile clubs that do not demand the exact striking accuracy of a long iron. I have written about how you can use them to their full advantage so that the beginner and the more experienced player alike can achieve maximum length from the fairway.

Most courses have trees, which more often than not seem to be between you and your target. In the chapter on trees, you will learn how to assess the best route to your target, either over, under, round or through, and also how to execute that shot. All courses have rough to some degree or another, and having gone into it you must aim to get out in one shot as accurately as possible. The chapter on the rough explains how to employ the correct technique to gain length when necessary, and control when around the green.

The last two chapters deal with special shots in the short game, namely playing to two-tiered and elevated greens. Every golfer can reduce a handicap considerably by improving his/her short game, and with the aid of the earlier chapters in this book which deal with sloping lies around the green and in bunkers, you should be able to add to your repertoire of short game shots.

Planning and executing the more difficult and unusual shots in golf can be very satisfying and rewarding, and no matter how good a golfer you are, you will not hit the middle of every fairway and every green. Moreover, in matchplay, a good shot from a tricky lie or around the trees will always give you the upper hand psychologically.

CHAPTER ONE

Downhill lies from the fairway

The most important point to consider when playing a shot from anything other than a flat lie is how to adjust your set up and how you can expect the ball to react. I firmly believe that a correct address position for whichever shot is to hand is essential if you are to play the shot well. However, the beginner may experience some problems remembering how to adjust the set up. Naturally, the longer you play, the easier it is to remember what to do, but it does surprise me how often even established club golfers seem to have little knowledge of how to cope with sloping lies.

Club selection

The first thing to consider is the severity of the slope and how that will affect your choice of club. Any downhill lie will de-loft the club, so that a 7 iron could be more like a 5 or 6 iron, depending on just how steep the slope is (Fig 1.1). If you have a very long shot, be careful about

Fig 1.1. On a downhill lie, the loft of the club is reduced so a 7 iron can become more like a 5 iron, depending on the severity of the slope

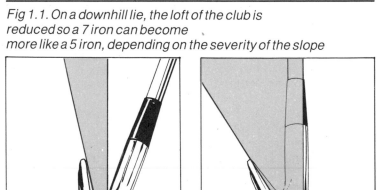

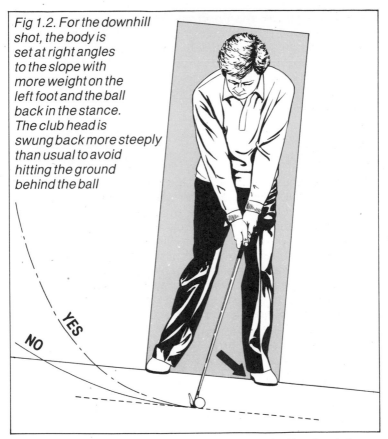

Fig 1.2. For the downhill shot, the body is set at right angles to the slope with more weight on the left foot and the ball back in the stance. The club head is swung back more steeply than usual to avoid hitting the ground behind the ball

selecting a 2 or 3 iron, since their reduced effective loft would make them extremely difficult to use. You would be better playing a 4 or 5 iron, which will effectively become more like a 3, or to consider using a lofted wood such as a 5 or 7 wood.

The set up

For the downhill shot, you are trying to set your body in the same relationship to the ground as for the level lie. Normally on a shot from a level lie, your spine is at right angles to the ground, so to retain that relationship for a downhill lie, you must allow your weight to be more on your left than right foot, with the right knee more flexed than normal to accommodate the change. Your shoulders will then be more parallel to the slope and the left will feel considerably lower than normal, which will help you to swing the club in the correct manner for the shot. You should position the ball back in the stance, which will help you to make good contact. Again, how far back depends on the severity of the slope, and a little experimentation on your part will help you to discover the necessary degree of adjustment.

The swing

The set up adjustments will help you to make the correct swing, but you must also understand what you are trying to achieve. If you were to take the club away from the ball in the normal manner, i.e. initially fairly low to the ground, because the ground behind the ball is higher than usual, it would obstruct the club's progress. Therefore, it is essential that you swing the club more upright in the backswing, following the line of the slope (Fig 1.2). Your set up will help to a great extent but you should always have a couple of practice swings so that you know just

Fig 1.3. After impact you should try to swing the club head down along the contour of the ground, allowing the right knee to be more active than usual

how upright the backswing needs to *feel* in order to avoid hitting the ground behind the ball. Having swung up the slope on the backswing, you must have the feeling of swinging down the contour of the slope through the impact zone, and for this to happen your right knee may need to be more active than normal (Fig 1.3). It is possible that you will finish off balance — in extreme circumstances even taking a step after having hit the shot. This it why it is essential to have a couple of practice swings so you know what to expect and can therefore balance your body accordingly.

The ball's flight

Since the backswing will be more upright than normal, you will not turn your body as much which, together with the fact that you start with more weight on the left leg, means that you will not transfer as much weight to the right side as usual.

Consequently it is very easy for the left side to be a little ahead of its usual position at impact, and indeed the slope makes it easy for the left side to move out of the way. This action tends to leave the hands and arms behind, which can cause the club face to be open at impact, resulting in a shot that curves to the right. The situation is made worse by the fact that the ball is positioned back in the stance, which tends to send it to the right. So in extreme circumstances, you can get a shot that starts right of target and then curves even further to the right. You must allow for this by aiming to the left and trying not to let yourself move ahead of the shot. Feel that the swing is made primarily with your arms, allowing your legs to work at the moment of impact so that you can swing the club head down the slope. The ball will also fly lower than normal for the club you are using.

Summary

Be conservative with your choice of club; do not make the shot more difficult by taking a 3 wood or a 3 iron. Remember also that the ball will fly lower and will be inclined to go right of the target. Put more weight on the lower foot and the ball nearer to the high. Swing within yourself and try to remain balanced.

CHAPTER TWO

Downhill shots around the green

These are the shots when the ball is on a mound surrounding the green, quite often sitting down in the grass, which has prevented it from rolling back onto the green. At the best of times, shots from around the green require a delicate touch, but when your balance is affected by the slope and the ball's lie is less than perfect, then producing an action that makes ideal contact with the ball is relatively difficult. Perhaps the secret, if there is one, is to know how to allow and adjust for the slope's effect on the outcome of the shot and, of course, to practise.

Which club

Your choice of club will be affected by the severity of the slope and how much green lies between you and the hole. More often than not you will be near the edge of the green, but judging just how far the ball will run is mariginally more difficult than normal. As with the downhill lie on the fairway, whichever club you choose will have less effective loft so a 9 iron could be more like a 7 iron. Therefore, since you need to be able to control the shot, and unless you have perhaps 30 to 40 yards to the pin, I would suggest that you use either a wedge or a sand wedge for this shot. If you are, say, 30 yards away, then perhaps a 9 iron may be better so that the ball will roll most of the way to the hole. Whereas the downhill lie will send the ball lower, whenever you chip to a green below you the ball will not run as much as usual, which will help you to control the shot better. Take this into account before selecting your club and deciding how hard to hit the shot. Practice will help to cultivate your visualization of just what will happen to the ball.

The set up and swing

As with the shot from the fairway, you must try to set your spine at right angles to the slope by putting more weight on your left side, flexing your right knee more and playing the ball nearer to the right foot than normal. You

Fig 2.1. Set up with your spine at right angles to the slope, weight mainly on the left leg and the right more flexed than usual. With the ball back in the stance, the swing follows the contours of the ground

will find that a wider stance than you usually employ will give you a more secure and balanced set up (Fig 2.1).

Aim yourself left of target, grip down the club, even to the extent of placing the right hand on the shaft if necessary, and open the face of the club a little so that you have more effective loft to play with. Make the swing, mainly using just your hands, picking the club head up abruptly in the backswing to avoid the ground behind the ball. Keep the blade open through impact and do not let the grass twist it shut. This is a delicate shot so do not rush it — stay down after impact and try to swing the club head down the slope. Avoid all temptations to see the results of your efforts too soon as this will make you come up off the ball, most likely thinning it or leaving it on the bank.

11

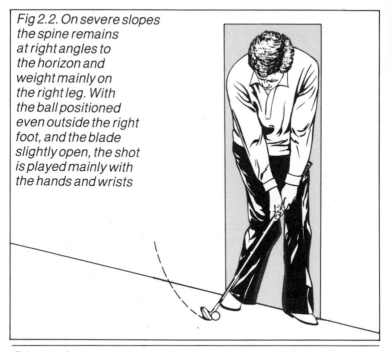

Fig 2.2. On severe slopes the spine remains at right angles to the horizon and weight mainly on the right leg. With the ball positioned even outside the right foot, and the blade slightly open, the shot is played mainly with the hands and wrists

Shots from severe slopes

You may have to play shots from such severe slopes that it is not possible to lean away from the slope without falling over. In these situations, try to adopt an address position that is as balanced as possible, which enables you to make the best contact under the circumstances. You will have to set your spine more at right angles to the horizon and may well find that your right leg is extremely bent. Aim left of target and play the ball well back in the stance, even outside the right foot so that you are able to hit the ball first instead of the ground (Fig 2.2). You will have to grip down on the club, perhaps even onto the shaft itself, and because of the ball's position, the club will have reduced effective loft causing the ball to fly much lower than normal. You can, of course, open the blade a little to gain extra height on the shot but on the severest of slopes, you will still have less loft on the club than from a flat lie.

For this shot, the swing is made just with the wrists and hands chopping down on the ball, so an accurate shot, especially from a bad lie, can be difficult to judge.

CHAPTER THREE

Downhill bunker shots

This is one of the most difficult and therefore most feared shots in golf. When the ball is on a downhill lie, it is usually near the back of the bunker, possibly with the lip of the bunker impeding the backswing, and thus you are confronted by two problems:

1 The downhill lie makes it more difficult to get sufficient height on the ball that it at least gets onto the green, even though it may be some distance from the pin.

2 Because the ball is often near the back of the bunker, the over-hanging lip can make it difficult to make an unimpeded backswing.

Consequently, there may be circumstances when it would be more prudent to settle for the green than to play towards the pin. Alternatively, if the shot is really fearsome, your best route may even be sideways or backwards — better to be out of the bunker with the first shot than to attempt the impossible and take several shots.

Fig 3.1a. When the blade of the sand iron is opened, the flange comes into play, preventing the club from digging too deeply into the sand b. When the blade stays square, the club digs deeper into the sand

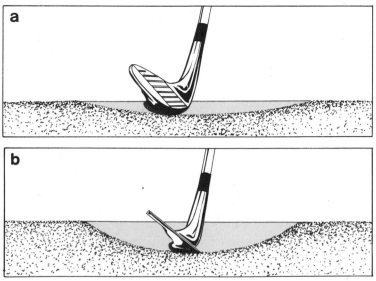

The set up

As with the other downhill shots you are trying to set your spine at right angles to the slope so that you avoid hitting the ground, or in this case the sand, behind the ball. So set up slightly open with more weight on the left leg than normal, the right knee well flexed and your shoulders virtually parallel to the sand (Fig 3.2). Position the ball more centrally than for a flat lie and grip down on the club, but do not open the blade too wide. The sand iron has a flange which is designed to stop the club digging too far into the sand. Instead it produces more of a skimming action (Fig 3.1). The wider the blade is opened,

Fig 3.2. With more weight on the left side, and the ball back in the stance, the backswing must be steep to avoid hitting the sand and the lip, so the wrists are cocked early as the arms swing up

the more the flange comes into play. However, when the ball sits on a downhill lie, there is more sand to penetrate behind it. Therefore, if you open the blade wide and bring the flange into play, you will make it more difficult to hit down through the sand. But because the downhill lie reduces the effective loft of a club, you may be tempted to open the blade to offset this. Weigh up the situation carefully, trying to balance the height needed on the shot by how much sand lies behind the ball. Again by experience and practice you will get to know just how much you can afford to open the face and still hit down through the sand without thinning the ball. If the bunker face is not too steep and the pin is set 25 yards away, you have no real problems. If the bunker face is steep and the pin is just 10 yards away, then you do have problems and will just have to accept that the ball may not finish near the hole. Getting the ball out with the first shot is your main objective.

The swing

You must swing your hands and arms up steeply away from the ball so that you do not hit the sand (Fig 3.2). Although you cannot take a proper practice swing in a bunker, I would suggest that you have a couple of practice backswings, just so that you can judge and feel how steep it needs to be. On very steep slopes, you may well have to break your wrists and even bend the left elbow as the first movement to avoid hitting the sand. Try to hit the sand about 2 inches behind the ball, and be absolutely certain to hit down and through, trying to follow the contour of the sand. Do not allow the right hand and arm to overpower the left which will close the club face. Instead, keep the left hand and arm accelerating, following the contour of the sand so that at the finish, the back of the left hand faces more towards the sky than the ground. Allow your knees to move towards the target as you strike the ball, which will help you to stay down through the shot (Fig 3.3). Whatever happens, do not be tempted into trying to scoop the ball out of the bunker; keep your hands leading the club head and trust the loft of the club. You will not finish with as full a follow through as on a normal shot — instead, your hands will probably finish about hip height and you might well be a bit off balance, but this does not matter if the

Fig 3.3. After impact the club must swing down the slope, so make sure the right knee moves towards the target

ball is out of the bunker. The ball will come out lower than usual and consequently run more on landing.

Summary

The most important point about this shot is to be realistic in what you can hope to achieve. Do not regard it as an admission of defeat to play out sideways or even backwards, I have seen top professionals do that, simply because they knew that to go for the pin or the green would be foolhardy. Spend some time practising the shot so that you can get used to the unaccustomed set up and the sort of action that is necessary for success.

CHAPTER FOUR

The uphill lie on the fairway

To most golfers this is an inviting lie and one that in certain circumstances can allow you to hit the ball a long way. If the ball settles on a slight uphill lie along a reasonably flat fairway, this is the time to hit a 3 wood or, in some cases, even a driver for the better golfer if maximum distance is needed. However, as with any shot from a lie other than level, adjustments need to be made and a good sense of balance maintained in order not to waste the inviting lie.

Club selection

An uphill lie will increase the effective loft on a club, thus turning a 5 iron into a 6 or even a 7, depending on the severity of the slope (Fig 4.1). Consequently the shot will tend to go higher and not as far as normal, so select a club with less loft. As already stated, if you have a long shot, provided that the slope is not severe and the ball is sitting up on a tuft of grass (what luck!), you can even hit a driver.

Fig 4.1. On an uphill lie the club becomes more lofted so that a 5 iron can become more like a 7 iron, depending on the severity of the slope

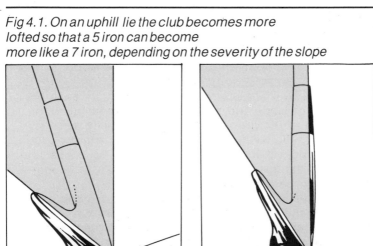

Fig 4.2. The spine is set at right angles to the slope, with more weight on the right leg and the left more flexed than normal. With the ball played more forward in the stance, the club head is swung along the contour of the slope as much as possible

The set up and swing

Following the same principle as for the downhill lie, you need to set your spine at right angles to the slope, so put more weight on your right leg and flex your left leg more than usual (Fig 4.2). This will bring your shoulders more parallel to the slope and thus enable you to swing along the contour of the ground. If you do not make this adjustment, you will just dig the club head into the ground at impact and not strike the ball very well. To ensure that you sweep the ball from the turf, position it a little nearer the left foot than for a flat lie.

As you swing the club head away, do not swing it up too steeply but try to swing down the slope. You will find it easy to make a good turn in the backswing and will have a lot of weight on the right leg at the top of the backswing. The main problem arises in trying to move your legs and hips through the shot sufficiently. Consequently, the arms and shoulders can tend to overtake them (Fig 4.3), creating a pull, draw or hook shot, so allow for this by aiming to the right at address. The practice swing will help you to gauge just how aggressive you can be with the shot and still remain balanced.

Alternatively, where accuracy rather than length is important, play the ball more centrally in the stance and restrict the backswing somewhat by making it mainly with the arms. Through the impact zone, concentrate on moving your legs and holding your hands squarer, preventing the right hand and arm from rotating over the left.

To help you remember how to adjust for uphill and downhill lies from the fairway, this short rhyme might help you.

'From an uphill or a downhill lie,
Weight to the low foot, ball to the high'

If you have trouble thinking of that, remember that 'weight' and 'low' both contain a 'W'.

Fig 4.3. Through impact it is difficult to transfer your weight back to the left side, and so the hands and arms tend to close the club face, creating a shot that goes left of target

CHAPTER FIVE

Uphill lies around the green

Just how accurate you can be with these shots will depend usually on how good a lie you have. Because the ball has remained on the slope, inevitably the grass may not be very short and so the ball may be lying badly, which makes the shot more difficult to judge. You may either hit a shot that flies out of the grass, or one that is rather dampened by the grass and falls short of the target. You have to decide, depending on how much grass will be between the blade and the ball at impact, which is more likely to happen. Having said that, from this lie you should be able to hit a reasonably good shot onto the green since it will not be difficult to get height on the ball, which means it will land fairly softly. However, you may have to deal with this shot in two different ways, depending on the severity of the slope.

Club selection for gentle slopes

On the uphill lie, where the degree of slope still permits you to set your spine at right angles to the slope, effective loft is added to the club so that the ball will go higher. A 9 iron might be more like a wedge so you can use either a less lofted club for the shot, or just make sure that you hit the ball sufficiently hard. Usually from an uphill lie, you are playing to a green above you, and whenever this happens the ball will run more. Luckily the additional loft that you can expect from the shot will help to control the ball, which, if the hole is cut close to you, will be most welcome. Club selection will depend on how much green you have to play with, and how you *feel* and *see* the shot.

The set up and swing for gentle slopes

Again, set yourself as much at right angles to the slope as possible, with more weight on the right foot, the left knee well flexed and the ball just forward of centre in your stance (Fig 5.1). Grip down on the club for extra feel and control, and make the swing with the hands and arms. There is no need to break the wrists too much on the

20

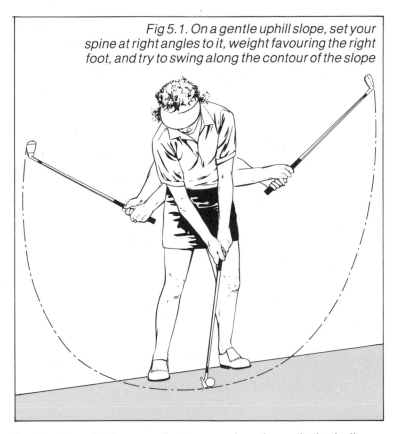

Fig 5.1. On a gentle uphill slope, set your spine at right angles to it, weight favouring the right foot, and try to swing along the contour of the slope

backswing. Make sure that you swing through the ball, allowing the club head to swing along the contour of the slope. However, take care that you do not swing *up* too much on the shot and thin the ball. Try to stay balanced and keep the eyes focused on the spot where the ball was a little longer than usual to prevent coming up too soon.

If you are faced with this shot and the ball is sitting on a tight lie, I would suggest that unless you are a very low handicap player, you should play the shot as described for the steep uphill shot which follows — otherwise, you could easily thin the shot.

Club selection for steep uphill slopes

On steep slopes you will not be able to add effective loft to the club face by your set up, since you will have to lean into the slope rather than away from it. But you can add loft by opening the club face at address, thus increasing the height of the shot. Most of the time you will need to use a wedge or sand wedge for this shot. Since you need height to clear the slope in front of you, if length is also needed you must consider the angle of the slope before deciding to hit a less lofted club.

The set up and swing for a steep slope

The severity of the slope will prevent you from setting yourself at right angles to it without falling over! Instead you must lean into the hill with your spine virtually perpendicular to the horizon, setting more weight on the left leg and also flexing it more than usual (Fig 5.2). You will have to grip down the club considerably, even onto the shaft in some cases, which may also prevent you hitting this shot very far. The ball is played just forward of centre. Do not attempt to swing down the slope in the backswing — just swing your hands and arms back quite naturally. Through the impact zone, feel that you are dragging the club head into the ball, keeping your hands ahead of the club head throughout the shot. The club head will tend to dig straight into the bank so be sure to keep a firm grip. The ball will still go high, but if it has been in a grassy lie it will lack backspin and will run on landing.

Tips for the higher handicaps

Newcomers to golf and higher handicap players usually attempt to hit a ball into the air by trying to scoop or lift it. First you must dismiss any thoughts of scooping or lifting from your entire approach to the game. The ball flies into the air by applying backspin, which is attained by striking *down* on the ball. Any time you try to hit up on the ball with an iron, you will impart topspin, which is what makes the ball nosedive along the ground. When faced with any shot from an uphill lie, because of the particular set up where the spine is virtually at right angles to the slope, there is a sense of hitting up on the ball. If you are someone who tends to thin shots in these instances, I would suggest that for all the shots around the green from uphill lies, you set your spine at right angles to the horizon with more weight on your left leg. This set up will help to guarantee a downward strike, and although the ball will not go as high as it would when set up at right angles to the slope, it will help you to strike correctly and produce a very satisfactory shot. By opening the club face a fraction before gripping the club, you will get extra height on the shot. Once you can master the shot from this set up, then, where the slope and lie permit, you can progress to tilting your spine at right angles to it and you will find that the ball will go higher and land softer.

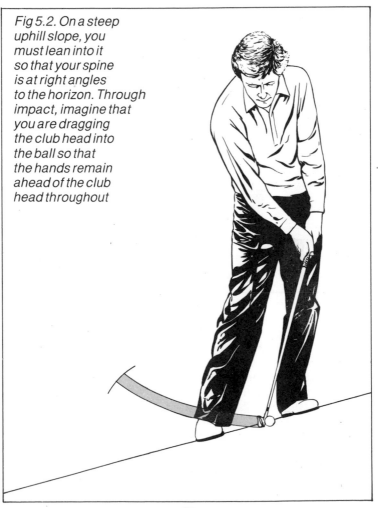

Fig 5.2. On a steep uphill slope, you must lean into it so that your spine is at right angles to the horizon. Through impact, imagine that you are dragging the club head into the ball so that the hands remain ahead of the club head throughout

Uphill bunker shots

Having now read five chapters on downhill and uphill lies, I hope that you will have a clear idea of how to hit this shot. You should by now have a much better picture of how the set up and the resultant swing should look. However, I have no intention of denying you a description of how the uphill bunker shot should be tackled, so read on!

The set up

Once more you must set your spine at right angles to the slope so that there will be more weight on the right foot than usual, the left leg will flex more, and the right shoulder will feel considerably lower than the left (Fig 6.1). On short shots, set up slightly open to the target but stand squarer for the long shots. You will naturally have more effective loft on the sand iron, so depending on the steepness of the bunker face, you may not have to open the club face as much as you think. Position the ball just inside the left heel.

The swing

Your set up will now allow you to swing along the contour of the sand with your normal bunker shot swing. Let the club head enter the sand about 2 inches behind the ball, and have the feeling of swinging up the slope (Fig 6.2a). The ball will come out higher and land more softly than usual so you will have to hit it harder, and also take less sand for longer shots. On severe slopes you may fall backwards after the shot so be sure to maintain your balance long enough to hit the shot well.

One of the most common mistakes is to bury the club head too deeply into the sand, which usually results in leaving the ball in the sand (Fig 6.2b). This occurs because the player fails to set up correctly — instead of leaning away from the slope, he/she leans into it. The correct set up dictates that you swing along the line of the slope, i.e. down in the backswing and up on the through swing,

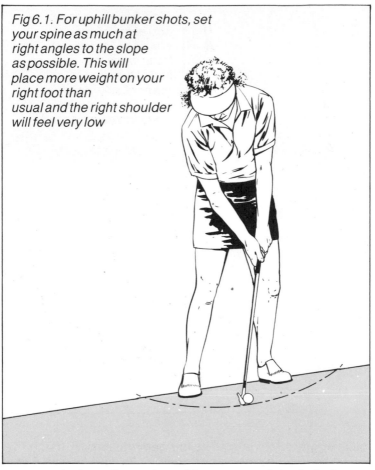

Fig 6.1. For uphill bunker shots, set your spine as much at right angles to the slope as possible. This will place more weight on your right foot than usual and the right shoulder will feel very low

taking a shallow divot of sand from around the ball. So do not argue with the slope; swing along it!

Playing from severe uphill lies

If the ball is on a severe slope, and this often occurs when the ball is near the top of the bunker face, then you may not be able to adopt the above set up and remain balanced. In this case you must lean into the slope so that most of your weight is on your left foot and the ball is fractionally more central in your stance. Open the club face a little to ensure that you have sufficient loft for the ball to clear the lip of the bunker and then swing the club

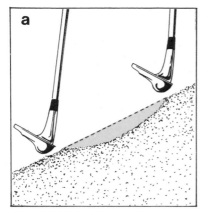

Fig 6.2a. When set up correctly, you will be able to swing the club head along the line of the sand on the backswing and throughswing, taking a shallow divot of sand

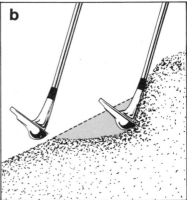

Fig 6.2b. If you fail to set up correctly there is every chance you will bury the club into the sand probably leaving the ball in the bunker

quite aggressively into the sand behind the ball, trying to swing through as much as possible. As already explained, the extra amount of sand beyond the ball will make it difficult for you to swing through very far and the whole action will feel like a stabbing motion.

Summary

However many words are written on the subject, you will only learn exactly how to tackle less straightforward shots by playing them, so spend some time hitting shots from a variety of lies. Armed with the knowledge of how to play them, once you have successfully done so in practice, you will be more confident when faced with the shot on the course.

CHAPTER SEVEN

Fairway shots with ball below feet

This shot has to fall into the category of one of the least liked shots in golf. It is definitely not one to 'have a go' at. Indeed, caution must be the watchword or disastrous results may ensue. Whereas the uphill and downhill shots require a change in weight distribution at address in order to play them successfully, it is your posture that must be adjusted when the ball is above or below your feet. Since so many golfers fail to achieve good posture even for a shot from a level lie, it is no wonder that the sidehill shots, particularly when the ball is below the feet, cause so many problems.

Set up

When the ball is below your feet, it is further away from you than on a flat lie, so to compensate you stand closer

Fig 7.1. When the ball is below the feet, you must angle your spine forward by bending more at the hips and then flex your knees. You must have sufficient weight on your heels so that you remain balanced when you swing

to it and lower the club head down to it by bending forward more from the hips, making sure that you grip at the end of the club and flexing your knees a little more (Fig 7.1). You need an upright swing for this shot and thus it is essential that you increase the angle of tilt from your hips — just bending your knees will not provide the correct plane to the swing. You must be well balanced to prevent any possibility of falling forward when playing the shot, which could result in a shank. The severity of the slope will dictate weight distribution, and although you will feel more weight towards your toes than for a shot from a level lie, you must have sufficient weight towards your heels to prevent over-balancing. However, do avoid sitting back too much on your heels as this has a tendency to ruin the correct spinal angle necessary for the shot. It is best to establish that you have a secure stance by having a couple of practice swings, which will also enable you to find out how hard you can safely hit the shot and remain balanced. You can improve the strike also by playing the ball nearer the centre of your stance. Be conservative on club selection — now is not the time to pull out a 3 iron — and be content with using mainly the middle irons, unless the slope is not too severe and the ball is sitting extremely well. If you need distance, use a 5 or a 7 wood.

The swing

You make the swing mainly with your hands and arms and there is little body turn (Fig 7.2). This, combined with the fact that the set up demands that the swing is upright, will inevitably lead to an out-to-in swing path causing the ball to fade, so aim left to allow for this (Fig 7.3). Swing at no more than three-quarter pace or length, and try to stay down through the shot for as long as possible. On steep slopes you may even fall right off balance after the strike, so do not swing too aggressively. The fading flight of the ball, plus the three-quarter length swing, will naturally restrict the distance the ball goes, so always balance your choice of club between what you can safely expect to hit from the lie and the distance to the hole.

Fig 7.2. The backswing should be made mainly with the arms, and because of the set up and lack of body turn, it will be quite upright, setting the swing on an out-to-in path

Fig 7.3. Like the backswing, the follow through will also be upright and three-quarter length. The out-to-in swing path will cause the ball to fade

CHAPTER EIGHT

Ball below feet around the green

As with the shot from the fairway, maintaining your balance will help you to hit this shot well. Perhaps it is because it is one of the least common shots that you may be called upon to play that makes this shot even more difficult. Setting up in a balanced position so that you can swing the club back without hitting your right knee with the shaft is often the main problem.

Set up and swing

Because you are near the green, you are more likely to be using a short iron for this shot. So set up in a similar manner as for the shot from the fairway, standing closer to the ball and bending forward more from the hips with your knees sufficiently flexed (Fig 8.1) You should not

Fig 8.1. Grip down the shaft a little, bend forward from the hips and flex the knees more than usual to get the correct well balanced address position. Although your weight will slide towards your toes, you must have enough weight on your heels to remain balanced throughout the shot

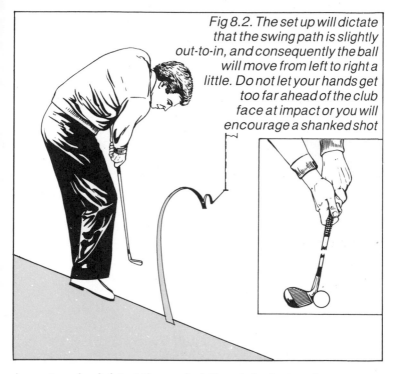

Fig 8.2. The set up will dictate that the swing path is slightly out-to-in, and consequently the ball will move from left to right a little. Do not let your hands get too far ahead of the club face at impact or you will encourage a shanked shot

have to grip right at the end of the club, but make sure that you are comfortably balanced. Depending on the severity of the slope, your weight will be forced towards the toes and balls of your feet, but, as with the shot from the fairway, you must have sufficient on your heels to ensure good balance. Even with this short shot, the ball is likely to fade or go slightly right of your target so allow for this in your aim (Fig 8.2).

The swing is made purely with the hands and arms and, due to the set up, the club head is swung back and through on a slightly out-to-in path. As you swing the club head into the ball, do not let your hands get too far ahead of the club face or you may shank the shot (Fig 8.2 inset). However, you must keep both hands moving through impact so that the right hand and arm do not fold over the left. It would also be prudent to address the ball slightly more towards the toe end of the club rather than the middle, as this will give you a little more room for error should you fall forward at all. The most crucial point about the shot is to stay down throughout and try to listen for the ball landing before you raise your head or your spine.

CHAPTER NINE

Ball below feet in a bunker

This can be one of the most awkward shots to play since very often the ball will have come to rest at the edge of the bunker, thus preventing you from standing in the bunker to play the shot. However, you have to accept such difficulties as part of the challenge of the game, and instead of bemoaning your luck, you should concentrate and decide on the best way to tackle the shot.

Fig 9.1. When the ball is close to the edge of the bunker, you may have to stand outside it. You will then need to take a very wide stance and bend forward a long way in order to stand any chance of getting the ball out

The set up

One way that you can help to off-set the ball being below
your feet is by working your feet into the sand more than
usual. This will naturally lower you towards the ball even
though you might get sand in your shoes! Having done
that, you must make the same adjustments for this shot as
for the others with this stance, i.e. stand closer to the ball,
bend sufficiently from the waist, grip a little nearer the end
of the club than usual and get yourself well balanced.
With most bunker shots you aim left of target so that you
can swing from out-to-in, but since this particular stance
encourages an out-to-in swing anyway, do not aim
yourself too far left. Instead, have the club face just open
and position the ball nearer the centre of your stance than
for a bunker shot from a flat lie. If the ball is so close to
the left edge of the bunker that you have to stand outside
to play it, you just have to take your stance as best you
can. It may mean that you have to spread your feet very
wide apart, and bend forward more (Fig 9.1) or, if you can
somehow get one foot in the bunker, kneel with the other
leg. Take your time over this, and have a few practice
swings *without touching the sand,* until you feel that you
are in the best possible position. Should you decide that
to try to play the ball towards the pin is beyond your
capabilities, then play sideways or backwards — *this is not
accepting defeat,* but using your head wisely. All that
anyone is really interested in is the final score, so better to
get out in one shot than try to accomplish the shot of the
century and need several attempts.

The swing

If the ball is not too far below your feet, then you can
expect the shot to be as good as one from a flat lie. But
realising your limitations in golf is sometimes one of the
harder lessons to learn, and if the ball is considerably
below your feet or you are having to stand outside the
bunker, then do not expect miracles. Be satisfied with
getting the ball out with the first shot (hopefully in the
direction of the hole) but if the pin is quite a distance
away, you may be wiser to concentrate on just getting out
rather than going for distance. On severe slopes, the more
effort you put into this sort of shot, the more likely you are
to mishit it. The swing is made with the hands and arms,

with the wrists breaking immediately the backswing starts.
This usually happens because the sand behind the ball is
quite steep and you must avoid hitting it. Thus the
backswing is very upright. The club head should enter the
sand about 2 inches behind the ball, and through impact
you *must* keep down through the shot. Try to imagine
that the club head is going underneath the ball and
coming out of the sand about 4 or 5 inches ahead of
where the ball was. Concentrate on this rather than being
too keen to see the results of your efforts (Fig 9.2). You
must retain the same angles of your knees and back that
you set at address; if you rise up at all you will most likely
play the next shot from the same bunker. Do not allow the
right hand to cross over the left, which would close the
club face. Concentrate instead on accelerating both hands
through the shot. You may fall off balance once you have
hit the ball but this is of no consequence — just make sure
that you keep your balance long enough to hit the ball.
Try to make the swing as smooth and unhurried as
possible.

Fig 9.2. So that you remain down long
enough on the shot, try to imagine
that the club will exit the sand
about 4 to 5 inches ahead of where
the ball lies. The set up will
restrict your shoulder turn and
encourage a full wrist
cock in the backswing

CHAPTER TEN

Ball above feet
on the fairway

As long as the slope is not too steep, this can be one of
the more inviting shots in golf and tends to encourage a
good attacking swing. So often the beginner fails to make
a good shoulder turn in the swing, producing instead a
rather weak 'arms only' type of action. When the ball is
above your feet, it encourages a good shoulder turn and
consequently a more powerful shot is the result. So if the
lie is not too extreme, you can look for a good shot. If you
are unlucky enough to find the ball considerably above
your feet, then you may have to sacrifice power for
accuracy, depending on what lies ahead.

Now that you understand how to compensate for the
ball being below your feet, you can understand also how
best to play those shots from above your feet. In fact, we
tend to make almost exactly opposite compensations, so
if you can remember how to play the shots below your
feet, then you need only try to make the reverse
alterations.

*Fig 10.1. When the ball
is above your feet, keep
your spine more erect,
grip down a little on the
club and make sure you
are well balanced with
a little more weight
towards your heels*

35

The set up

When the ball is above your feet, it is closer to you than
on a flat lie. Therefore, you will not need to bend from the
hips as much as usual in order to ground the club.
Consequently your spine will be more erect, with more
weight on your heels than on a level lie (Fig 10.1).
However, do not lean away from the hill but feel that your
spine is more at right angles to the horizon than normal.
Depending on the severity of the slope, you may like to
grip down on the club a little, so that the swing does not
become too flat. If the ball is only slightly above your feet
you can probably play it in its usual position, but where
the slope is steep, play it nearer the centre of your stance.
You can be quite attacking with this shot, and very often a
wooden shot is most successful since its rounded sole will
adapt better to the lie.

The swing

Because of your erect spine and the fact that the ball is
above your feet, the plane of the swing will be flatter than
normal. You will be more aware of the rotary movement
of the body and, indeed, the hands and arms will swing on
a flatter plane as well (Fig 10.2). These changes should
occur naturally and you would be wrong to try to prevent
them. Take a couple of practice swings so that you know
how the swing will feel. It is almost as though the ball was
teed on a very high tee-peg, where you would have to
swing more horizontally in order to strike it correctly. At
the top of your backswing, you will feel that your arms are
more behind your head than normal, and likewise on the
throughswing, they will finish more around your body
than above your head (Fig 10.3). The outcome is a swing
path that is more in-to-in than normal, resulting in a shot
that is liable to draw or even hook, so aim right to allow
for this. If you want to hit the ball hard but need a fairly
straight shot, you could either open the club face a little at
address or hold your hands squarer through the shot,
preventing the right hand and arm rotating over the left. If
you allow the ball to draw, it will fly lower than normal and
run on landing so you can probably play one less club than
usual.

If the lie is rather severe, you will have to make a more

controlled three-quarter length swing. Always take a couple of practice swings, which will help to tell you how aggressive you can be and still maintain your balance.

Fig 10.2. The set up will mean that the backswing is flatter than usual, with the hands and arms more behind than above your head. This creates an exaggerated in-to-in attack on the ball

Fig 10.3. The through swing must also be flatter with the hands and arms finishing lower than usual. The ball is liable to draw or hook, so allow for this by aiming to the right

CHAPTER ELEVEN

Ball above feet around the green

This shot is usually played from a mound around the green, invariably onto a green below the ball. Unfortunately, it is not always easy to be accurate with this shot, especially if the ball is lying badly. The very set up encourages a shot that is hard to control, and the prospect of the ball lying poorly adds another difficult factor to the shot. Whilst you should always be able to get the ball onto the green, the degree of difficulty of stance and lie may mean that getting the ball close to the hole can be something of a lottery. Furthermore, many golfers will not necessarily experience playing this sort of shot very often, especially if you play most of your golf on a well manicured parkland course. Those golfers who play links-type coastal courses will undoubtedly be faced with this type of shot quite regularly and will therefore know more about its problems.

The set up and swing

As with the shot from the fairway, your spine is more erect than normal, so much so that for extreme examples of this shot where the ball might be about waist high, you are standing almost totally upright. You will always have to grip down the club, sometimes with both hands on the shaft rather than the grip. Your weight will be more towards your heels but you will feel quite a strain at the front of your shins since your feet are likely to be angled upwards. You will feel as though you are leaning more towards the slope than away from it, and be certain that you have a secure footing for although the shot may not require much force, your body and stance need to remain as steady as possible. Position the ball near the centre of your stance.

The shot is played with the hands and arms, with the club being swung fairly horizontally depending on the degree of slope (Fig 11.1). If the grass is cut short the shot is not too difficult, but if you are in short rough you may need to pick the club up with your hands in the backswing to avoid catching the club in the grass. You must feel as though you are dragging or pulling the club head back into the ball so that you attain the same impact position as you had at address, with the hands ahead of the club face. The wrists need to stay firm through the impact zone so that you feel the forearms rather than the hands swinging the club, and you keep the blade in a square or open position, never letting it close. In a very bad lie, the grass can easily twist the club face closed which will cause an inaccurate shot, so be very firm with the left hand and do not let the right roll over the left. In most instances, the ball is likely to be pulled, so aim slightly right of target.

Fig 11.1. When the ball is very much above your feet, your spine is virtually straight. To help control the shot, grip well down on the club. The flat swing will make you pull or hook the ball left, so aim right to allow for this

CHAPTER TWELVE

Ball above feet
in a bunker

Although this shot is not so formidable as the ball below
the feet shot, nevertheless it is not always as easy as it
seems. Greenside bunker shots are best played using a
rather steep out-to-in swing, which produces a shot that
flies high without too much run on landing. However, as
explained in the previous two chapters, when the ball is
above the feet it produces a flatter in-to-in shaped swing.
For bunker shots this can make it rather difficult to
contact the sand at the predetermined spot, resulting in a
shot that is not as good as might have been expected.

The set up and swing

If the slope is gentle and the ball is not too much above
your feet, I would suggest that you stand a little further
away from the ball and set up with your body aimed left of
the target as for a normal bunker shot and the blade just
open. Do not wriggle your feet too deeply into the sand
but grip a little further down on the club to prevent it
digging too deeply into the sand. The gentle slope will not
prevent you swinging your arms up in the backswing,
which means you will make an adequately steep swing
and provided that you do not allow the right hand to roll
over the left through impact you should be able to hit a
shot that does not roll too much on landing. As the club is
shorter than normal, you may have to hit the shot slightly
harder than from a flat lie.

Where the ball is considerably above your feet, you
make the same adjustments as for the fairway shot, i.e.
stand more upright and further from the ball so that your
arms are slightly extended, grip down on the club and play
the ball nearer the centre of your stance. Since the lie will
encourage a shot that hooks or pulls, you should aim right
of target and maintain a fairly square set up with your feet
and shoulders. Do not dig your feet into the sand too
much as this will make you even lower than the ball, but
do make certain that your stance is secure. Open the
blade as appropriate for the shot so that you get enough
height on the ball. As I have already explained, the swing
for this shot will be flatter than usual, and you should

allow for this action rather than fighting it. While your arms and body turn more horizontally in the backswing, allow your wrists to break. On the downswing feel as though your arms are pulling or dragging the club head back into the sand — do not throw the club head at the sand with your hands as you will only strike the sand too far behind the ball. You will feel that your body is turning through the shot more than usual, and due to the flatter plane, you may find that your hands and arms want to rotate to the left through impact. This will tend to shut the club face causing the ball to come out lower than usual with right to left spin on it so that it will run on landing.

You must concentrate on the spot where you wish the club head to enter the sand and be certain to swing right through the shot. If you find that you are taking too much sand before the ball, adjust your intended entry point closer to the back of the ball. The fact that you have gripped down on the club may mean that you need to hit the ball harder, but this factor can be offset if the ball has a little draw flight on it and thereby runs more on landing.

Bunker shots from flat and perfect lies need to be practised in order for the ball to land near the pin each time, so do not expect these more difficult bunker shots to land where you want them without practising regularly.

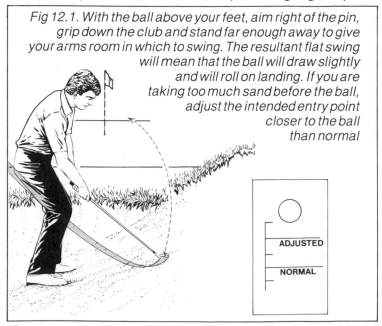

Fig 12.1. With the ball above your feet, aim right of the pin, grip down the club and stand far enough away to give your arms room in which to swing. The resultant flat swing will mean that the ball will draw slightly and will roll on landing. If you are taking too much sand before the ball, adjust the intended entry point closer to the ball than normal

ADJUSTED

NORMAL

CHAPTER THIRTEEN

Making full use of fairway woods

Certainly for the beginner and probably for the majority of club golfers, the long irons are the hardest clubs to hit. The small bladed heads of the 1, 2, 3 and 4 irons do not immediately inspire confidence. Added to this, the longer shafts in these clubs can tend to make them more unwieldly, and their lack of loft only exaggerates unwanted sidespin. So often the shots with these clubs are poor which leads to lack of confidence, resulting in the golfer thrashing at the ball in a most unco-ordinated fashion. Something of a stigma was once attached to the player who *resorted* to using a 5 wood instead of a long iron, but in recent years this trend and thinking has been reversed, helped considerably by players like Lee Trevino extolling the value of the 5 and 7 woods. Fairway woods are versatile and their extra loft, compared to that of a long iron, will not create as much unwanted sidespin. With a good understanding of how they should be hit in specific circumstances, you also will be singing their praises.

Fairway woods from a good lie

When faced with a long shot from the fairway with the ball sitting up on a cushion of grass, you should be aiming to sweep the ball from the top of the grass, just taking a few blades of grass after the strike rather than a large divot. In order to sweep the ball away rather than hit down on it, you should position it opposite your stance at the point where the club reaches the bottom of its arc. Thus it will be slightly nearer the left foot than for iron shots and just back from where you would play your driver.

It is impossible to be definite about the exact point and you will need to experiment a little yourself, but with the ball somewhere just inside your left heel you should not be too far out (Fig 13.1a). Your weight should be about 50:50 on each foot, although if you are lucky enough to find an exceptionally good lie — sometimes this happens in light rough where the ball is really sitting up — you could put a *little* more weight on the right foot.

a

Fig 13.1a. Position the ball at the lowest point in the arc so that the ball is swept away from the turf. The arms and body move away together so that the clubhead is kept low to the ground at the start of the backswing

When viewed face on, your left arm and the shaft should form a relatively straight line, and the sole of the club should sit flat on the ground (Fig 13.1a). Many players make the mistake of raising the back edge of the club and hooding the face by getting their hands too far ahead at address. Although there are times when you may need an address position similar to this (which I will cover later), it does in fact encourage a steeper attack on the ball, which is not ideal for a good lie.

The wood should be swung on a fairly shallow, wide arc so that in the initial stages of the backswing you should feel your arms and shoulders swinging away *together*. Do not just swing the club head up in the air with your arms; try to keep it low to the ground at least until it has passed your right foot so that at the top of the swing you have made a full turn with your shoulders and your weight is predominantly on your right leg. As your arms swing down, you must sense that you are going to sweep the

43

club head into the back of the ball and continue into a full, well balanced finish.

Due to a certain lack of strength, and often poor technique, many lady golfers fail to strike iron shots crisply enough, failing to take a divot after the ball. Therefore, the gently sweeping action of their swings lends itself most appropriately to fairway wood shots, and they should maximize their use of these clubs.

Which club you use will depend naturally on the distance to be covered and the lie of the ball. Most sets these days include a 3 and 5 wood, but you will also find that more manufacturers are making 7 woods, which would be the equivalent of a 3 or 4 iron. To vary the distance you hit the woods, naturally you can change the amount of force in the swing, but also by gripping down the shaft you will find that you can play shots of a great variety of lengths. It would be a good exercise to hit some

b

Fig 13.1b. For a bad lie or in the rough, position the ball back in the stance but keep the hands ahead of the ball so that the back of the sole will be off the ground. Swing your arms and the club head up more steeply in the backswing to encourage a more downward attack on the ball

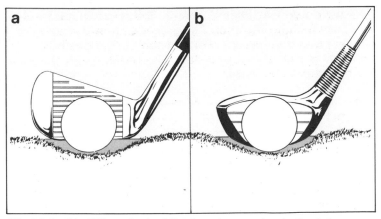

Fig 13.2a & b. When the ball lies in a depression in the fairway, the rounded soled fairway wood is better suited to the shot than the long bladed iron

4 irons on the practice ground and then use your 5 and 7 woods to try to cover the same distance. This will teach you how to conjure up shots by a combination of different grip positions, swing paces and lengths.

Fairway woods from the rough or a bad lie

If the ball is sitting in a slight depression on the fairway or sitting down a little in the rough, a fairway wood will almost always be the best club to use if you have a long distance to cover. On the fairway, the shape of the fairway wood is more suitable than the long blade of an iron (Fig 13.2), whilst in the rough the broad sole tends to flatten the grass out of its way, and the grass will not tangle around the wood like it does with an iron. Because the ball is sitting down, you will need a steeper angle of attack than for a good lie, so position the ball nearer the centre of your stance. This will allow your hands to be more ahead of the club head and the ball and encourage the steep attack. In this instance the club face might become slightly hooded with the back edge off the ground (Fig 13.1b). You may also need your weight to favour the left foot *slightly*, depending on just how bad the lie might be. As you swing the club head away, try to swing your arms a little more upright than usual, or if you are in the rough you may need to pick up the club head quite quickly with an early wrist break. Your downswing force will be directed downwards rather than forwards so that it feels more like a chopping than a sweeping action. I would not suggest that you use a 3 wood in such situations but depending on the lie and distance required, a 4, 5 or 7 wood should be ideal.

Woods from a bunker

If the ball is sitting well towards the back of a bunker that does not have a steep face, you can use a 5 or 7 wood to good effect. Take a firm stance but do not bury your feet too much in the sand, and grip down the club a little to compensate for the stance. Play the ball just forward of centre and, with a firm wristed swing, smoothly clip the ball from the top of the sand. Keep your arms swinging throughout the shot rather than trying to flick at the ball with your wrists, as you will more than likely hit the sand

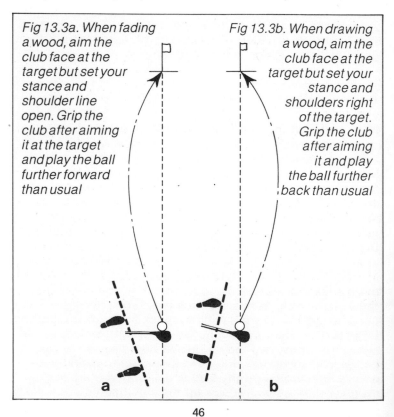

Fig 13.3a. When fading a wood, aim the club face at the target but set your stance and shoulder line open. Grip the club after aiming it at the target and play the ball further forward than usual

Fig 13.3b. When drawing a wood, aim the club face at the target but set your stance and shoulders right of the target. Grip the club after aiming it and play the ball further back than usual

before the ball. Looking at the top of the ball rather than at the back, may help you to hit it cleanly. If you catch the sand before the ball the shot is dampened and you might just as well have played more conservatively. This is not a shot for the beginner, and no matter what standard of golfer you may be, a little practice will tell you when to gamble and when to be less attacking. You will also find it an easier shot to hit from firm rather than soft sand.

Woods in the wind

If you are playing downwind, the woods will send the ball higher than their equivalent irons. For example, a 5 wood will hit the ball higher than a 2 iron so you will be able to take more advantage of the wind. Of course, the reverse might be true when playing into the wind, but provided that the lie is reasonable, a 3 or 4 wood will not hit the ball too high. If you grip down on the club with a firmer grip than usual, you will produce a firmer wristed swing that will hit the ball lower. Do not be tempted to hit the ball very hard as this usually results in more backspin and sends the ball higher. Whilst your companions may be happy hitting a 2 iron into the wind, in these circumstances any unwanted sidespin is accentuated and the ball needs to be struck quite purely. You would undoubtedly be better off playing a fairway wood in which you have confidence and which will tolerate a certain degree of mis-hit more readily than the long iron.

In cross winds it is better to aim off to allow for the wind rather than shaping the ball against the wind. But sometimes you may feel that in order to control the ball better, a certain amount of intended fade or draw would be an advantage. This really only applies to the better player — the higher handicap golfer should just allow for any crosswind in his/her aim.

Shaping the shots

If you need to fade a long shot with a wood, you will get better results from a 3 or 4 wood than the 5 or 7. When fading a shot the club face is open to the line of the swing, adding loft to the club face. The higher numbered woods already have more loft than the 3 or 4, and the additional loft added will make them more liable to add backspin and not sidespin to the shot. That is not to say that you cannot fade the 5 or 7, just that it is easier with a 3 or 4.

To fade or slice the ball you must align yourself and consequently the swing path left, i.e. out-to-in, in relation to the intended target, with the ball further forward in your stance than usual (Fig 13.3a). Thus a club placed across your shoulders should point left of the target and not parallel to it. Having set up in this position, just open the club face so that it points more towards the intended target, and then re-grip it so that your hands are in their normal position but the club face is open. The amount of

Fig 13.4a. When fading the ball, make certain that the left hand leads through impact and just beyond. You may need more leg action than usual to help keep the blade open

Fig 13.4b. When playing a draw, depending on how much the ball needs to curve, you may have to encourage the right hand and arm to rotate over the left through the impact zone

curve will depend on how far left you aim, and how far right the club face is positioned at impact. Do not allow the right hand and arm to cross over the left through the impact zone but keep the left in command throughout, allied to slightly more emphasis on your leg action (Fig 13.4a). The shot will go higher than normal and will not run much on landing. Thus you will lose some distance on the shot.

When you need to hook or draw the ball, you will find that you have more control with the more lofted woods. Trying to hook the 3 wood may result in a shot that barely gets off the ground or runs into trouble. When drawing or hooking a ball, the club face needs to be closed to the swing path, and consequently effective loft is deducted from the club face. Since the 4, 5 and 7 woods have a reasonable amount of loft already, they will be better suited to curving the ball from right to left in a controlled manner with the ball flying through the air and not along the ground.

To draw or hook the ball, aim yourself, and consequently the swing path right, i.e. in-to-out in relation to the intended target, with the ball further back in your stance than usual (Fig 13.3b). A club placed across your shoulders will point at or right of the target. Once set up, close the club face so that it faces more towards the target, then re-grip it so that your hands are in their normal position but the club face is closed. Again the amount of curve will depend on how much the club face is pointing to the left of the swing path at impact. You may need to encourage your right hand and arm to rotate over the left through the impact zone, depending on how much curve you need on the ball (Fig 13.4b). The ball will fly lower than usual for the club you are hitting and will roll on landing, thus gaining you some distance on the shot.

Summary

I hope you can now see how versatile your fairway woods can be. Ladies especially would benefit from making full use of their more lofted woods. Long irons do require a certain amount of strength to be struck properly, and the lady beginner rarely possesses the strength of hand or technique to feel totally at home with them. Be smart and get to know both your own and the clubs' capabilities, and the fairway woods will become your secret weapon.

CHAPTER FOURTEEN

Trees: over, under, round, through

Someone has created a rumour that trees are 75 per cent air. Ask any golfer if he/she agrees with that statement, and I am sure that the answer would be 'no'. Whilst not all courses have trees that come into play, it is inevitable that sooner or later you will play a course where trees are a considerable hazard. Having played a shot that puts a tree between you and the target, you must first decide which is the most sensible route either to the hole or back onto the fairway. I know that I may have written this already, but the wise golfer is one who knows his/her limitations. Luckily many professional tournaments are televized these days and we see international stars playing incredible shots from deep in the woods or around trees. Unfortunately, many golfers seek to emulate their heroes and, armed with the same intent but not the same ability, they too try to perform miraculous shots. If you do not escape from the trees at the first attempt, invariably the ball will hit a branch and can land up anywhere. Sadly 'anywhere' is often an unplayable lie from where you have little chance of even swinging the club. I would not like you to think that I believe in playing sideways or backwards onto the fairway whenever you find yourself in the trees. This would be far too defensive and would also deny you the thrill of planning and executing the best shot possible. So this chapter aims to help you decide which shot to choose and how best to play it.

How to assess the shot

The first point to check is the lie of the ball, which will have an important influence on which types of shots are possible.

1 If the ball is lying well in light rough or on the fairway, your choice is not really restricted with the only danger being that you may try to be over-ambitious. If you can strike the ball without too much grass getting between the blade and the ball, you should be able to shape the shot left or right. Hitting the ball high or low should pose no problems (Fig 14.1a).

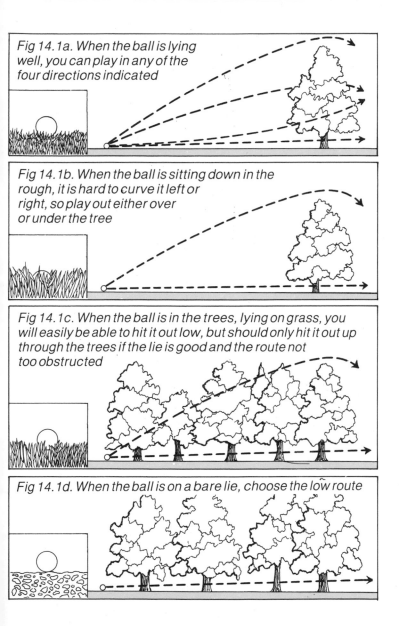

Fig 14.1a. When the ball is lying well, you can play in any of the four directions indicated

Fig 14.1b. When the ball is sitting down in the rough, it is hard to curve it left or right, so play out either over or under the tree

Fig 14.1c. When the ball is in the trees, lying on grass, you will easily be able to hit it out low, but should only hit it out up through the trees if the lie is good and the route not too obstructed

Fig 14.1d. When the ball is on a bare lie, choose the low route

2 If the ball is sitting down in the rough, you will have difficulties in curving it right or left, since too much grass will intervene between it and the blade. You may still be able to hit the ball high enough to get over the tree,

provided that it is not sitting down too deeply, whilst
hitting low will present no problems (Fig 14.1b).

3 If the ball is in the trees and lying in grass, for the
reasons given above you will not be able to curve it but
will be able to hit it high if the lie is not too bad and there
are no intervening branches. You will also be able to hit it
low (Fig 14.1c).

4 If you are in the trees and the ball is lying on bare earth,
you would be best advised to hit it out low. Only attempt a
lofted shot if there are no intervening branches and to hit
it low is impossible (Fig 14.1d).

The human factor

The options suggested above have not taken into account
your particular ability to hit each of the recommended
shots, and this is where you must be honest with yourself.
If you are an inveterate slicer, no matter how many words
I may write here on how to hook the ball around the trees,
you would be well advised not to attempt the shot without
first being able to produce it on the practice ground. If you
habitually move the ball from left to right, or vice versa,
always try to do what comes naturally, especially under
pressure. Accept that if you have never drawn or hooked
a ball in your life, wherever possible you should choose an
alternative shot to get yourself out of trouble until you
have had a chance to experiment on the practice ground.

The best tactical shot

Having outlined which shots are possible from different
lies, you must then consider which will be most
advantageous. If you choose to hit over the trees, you
may have no trouble hitting the ball high enough but can
you hit it far enough to clear the trees? It is always best to
have a look at the shot from the side so that you can see
just how far the ball must fly.

When playing a low shot from the trees, the main
danger can be hitting the ball too far so that it runs into
trees on the other side of the fairway (Fig 14.2). One can
easily be tempted into trying to 'make up' for the errant
shot and opt for as long a shot as possible. If you cannot

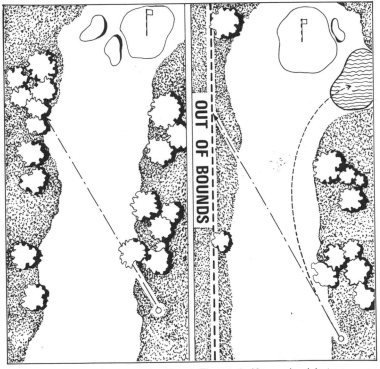

Fig 14.2. Do not be tempted to make up for a bad shot by being greedy for distance, since you might just hit the ball back into trouble

Fig 14.3. If you decide to curve the ball and do not hit it correctly, are you going to be in more trouble? In this example, if the ball does not fade enough, it could go out of bounds, whereas if it fades too much, it could land in the water

get the ball onto the green, you must look for the spot from which you would ideally like to play the next shot.

If you elect to fade the ball around the tree and do not manage to get the right amount of turn on it, are you likely to hit the ball out of bounds or into a lake or bunker (Fig 14.3)? Whilst you might have envisaged and have the opportunity to play this shot, the fact that if you over- or under-cut the ball will be disastrous may in itself prevent you from playing the shot to the best of your ability. You would be putting yourself under pressure, and only you know how well you can withstand pressure. A matchplay situation may demand different tactics from those employed in stroke play. This, together with your own particular form on the day, should help to determine how you tackle the shot.

Trying to play up through the trees perhaps presents the biggest chance of failure. It is easy to recall Severiano Ballesteros playing many superb shots from such positions, but remember that he is a genius and has the ability to match his attacking spirit for the game. He can execute such shots in the almost certain knowledge that he can play them successfully. If you are playing through the trees, you really must consider what might happen if you do not make good contact. Will the outcome be very costly or is it worth the gamble? If you have no alternative shot, okay, but consider this shot as a last option unless you are a very low handicap golfer with a good lie!

Fig 14.4. To hit a high shot, slightly open the club face and stance and play the ball forward. Put a little more weight on the right foot but do not set the hands too much ahead of the ball. In the backswing, allow the wrists to break early, as the arms swing up

The 'over' shot

This presupposes that the ball is sitting on a cushion of grass rather than bare ground. In this example, I will take it that the target, whether it is the green or a certain part of the fairway, is about 140 yards away and that you are at least 15 to 20 yards back from the tree. You must decide with which club you can best gain the required height and distance, remembering that the shot will not carry as far as usual as you will be hitting it higher.

Position the ball forward of centre, open the club face a little, aim slightly left of target and feel that your right shoulder is lower than usual. With a fairly narrow stance, keep your weight a little more on your right foot (Fig 14.4). These adjustments will help you to get height on the shot. At address keep your hands fairly level with the ball so that you can initiate the backswing with an early wrist break, which, together with the open stance, will help to create an upright swing and a steep attack on the ball. The shot will feel more 'handsy' than normal, but through impact you must not allow the right hand to cross over the left as this would de-loft the club face. Your arms should finish high. The length of shot, lie, height of the tree and your skill must together determine how long a club you can risk playing. You should practise with each club down to about your 5 iron to see how high and how far you can hit the ball. Only then will you really know whether you are taking a risk or are being sensible with your club and shot selection.

The 'under' shot

Since you want to play the ball out low, you should choose a club with little loft, perhaps anything between a 3 and a 7 iron. The problem you may face when playing a ball out low is that although you wish to avoid hitting overhead branches, you also want to clear any long grass or other obstructions lower down. A shot that travels almost completely along the ground may therefore not be the best choice. You may want one that flies about two feet off the ground, which may mean using a 6 or 7 iron depending on the lie and where you play the ball in your stance. Having selected the correct club, position it well back in your stance nearer your right foot to ensure keeping the ball low. This will reduce the effective loft of the club making a 7 iron react more like a 5 or 6 iron. Keep your hands well ahead of the ball so that the shaft slopes considerably towards the target, with your hands opposite your left thigh (Fig 14.5). Make sure that you keep the blade square, since with your hands so far forward it is easy to turn the blade open. With a wider stance than normal, place more weight on the left foot and make the swing in a firm wristed manner, feeling that you punch the ball out. Keep your hands ahead of the club at impact and beyond, finishing with the club head quite low to the ground. The ball will naturally run considerably so always have a couple of practice swings in order to judge the shot better.

The 'round' shots

In the last chapter I outlined how to shape shots with your fairway woods, and you would find it helpful to re-read that section of the book. However, if you have a shot of, say, 130 to 140 yards, you will not want a wood.

A shot of 130 yards that needs to curve from left to right, i.e. fade or slice, is best played with an iron that does not have too much loft. The fading family of shots requires a club face that is open to the swing path at impact, which consequently becomes more lofted and less likely to impart sidespin. To ensure that you get sidespin and not just additional backspin, select a straighter faced club, perhaps a 5 iron, and if necessary grip down on it and alter the length, pace and power of the swing to adjust the distance. Do not forget that a fading shot does not travel as far as a straight one. One of the pitfalls of this shot is not aiming sufficiently to the left at address. The path of the swing usually determines the initial direction of the ball, but when a club face is opened a lot, the ball will tend to start out between the line of the swing and where the club face is pointing. The set up is the same as for the fairway wood shot, but in the swing try to exaggerate the up-and-down movement of your arms. This action, together with keeping the body turn to a minimum in the backswing, will produce a more upright swing, which will encourage a fading flight on the ball (Fig 14.6). A firmer grip than usual will help to prevent unwanted hand action so that through impact you feel as though you are dragging the club head across the ball mainly with your arms, preventing the forearms from rotating anti-clockwise. The golfer who naturally slices all shots will probably not have to think too much about this shot but should just take care with aiming the shot. The golfer who naturally hooks or draws the ball will definitely need to observe the above points and make full use of a couple of practice swings to experience how the action should feel.

A shot of 130 yards that needs to curve from right to left may be played with a more lofted club than you would normally use from that distance, when the ball is required to hook or draw, the club face will have less loft on it than normal, so an 8 iron could be more like a 7 or 6 iron. Your set up will be similar to that described for shaping the fairway woods but do make certain that you aim enough to the right of the obstacle to avoid hitting it. Do not grip the club too tightly, and make a good shoulder turn in the

Fig 14.5. For a low shot, play the ball back in the stance, keeping the weight more on the left side, hands well ahead of the ball and the club face hooded. Make the swing very firm wristed, punching the ball out keeping the club head low to the ground after impact

backswing (Fig 14.7). Through impact feel that your hands and arms are rotating to the left. Your arms will finish more round your body than normal, and the ball will go further and lower than usual and run on landing, The golfer who naturally imparts draw or hook spin on the ball will not need to over-emphasise these points, but the slicer should take a couple of practice swings concentrating on allowing the hands and arms to be more active through the impact zone.

With each of these 'round' the tree shots, you should always assess whether you would be better off over-curving or under-curving the ball and let that dictate the degree to which you try to bend the shot.

Fig 14.6. When fading the ball with an iron, slightly restrict the shoulder turn and make a more upright arm swing. Make certain that you aim enough to the left as the open club face means the ball starts out just right of the swing path

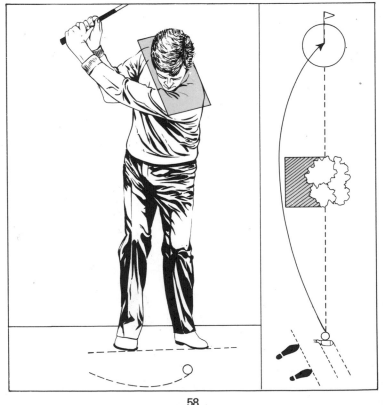

Fig 14.7. When drawing the ball, make a good shoulder turn and a flatter arm swing. Be sure to aim far enough to the right as the closed club face will make the ball start left of the swing path

The 'through' shot

For the high shot that emerges from a gap in the trees, you are more likely to use one of the short irons, and what you have to match is the angle at which the ball leaves the club with the gap through which you are planning to hit (Fig 14.8). If the lie is bare, the ball will fly lower, whereas a good lie will encourage height. Try to make the swing as smooth as possible and resist the temptation to look up or come up on the shot too early. Lining up the shot is crucial so do take time on this and use an intermediate target about a yard ahead of the ball to assist you.

If you are in the middle of the trees and decide to play out low, you may have to thread the ball between several trees to get back to the fairway. In this instance lining up is crucial since you may have only a few inches through which to squeeze the ball. As you will be playing the ball back in your stance, there is a chance that you could hit it slightly right of where you are aiming. You should either close the blade a little or aim a bit further left to compensate (Fig 14.9).

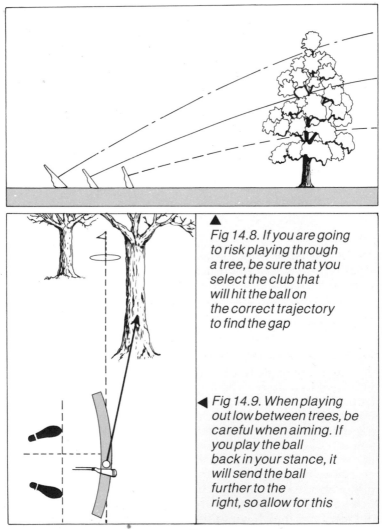

▲

Fig 14.8. If you are going to risk playing through a tree, be sure that you select the club that will hit the ball on the correct trajectory to find the gap

◀ Fig 14.9. When playing out low between trees, be careful when aiming. If you play the ball back in your stance, it will send the ball further to the right, so allow for this

CHAPTER FIFTEEN

Playing from the rough

It never ceases to surprise me how poorly many club golfers play shots from the rough. Possibly having hit what could at best be described as a 'weak' shot into the rough, they try to make up for the bad shot and proceed to take out their 3 wood and hit a ball that is barely visible. Then sadly, and inevitably, they take at least two or three more shots to move the ball anywhere near the fairway and thus pay the penalty for playing the wrong shot at the wrong time. There is no one club that is the correct one to use from rough — it will always depend on your lie, how far you have to go, how strong you are and what will happen if your chosen shot fails. In the chapter on trees, I highlighted how you must think about the shot and weigh up all the possibilities before you choose your club and exit route, and much the same advice applies to playing out of the rough. However, here are some points that are worth remembering next time you stray from the fairway.

Long shots from rough — club selection

The ideal club to gain maximum distance from the rough is a lofted wood. The loft on the same numbered woods does vary, and thus a 3 wood in one set may not have exactly the same loft as a 3 wood in another set but,

Fig 15.1. For long shots from rough, a fairway wood is usually the better club to use, since it glides through the rough, whilst the long grass wraps itself around the hosel of an iron

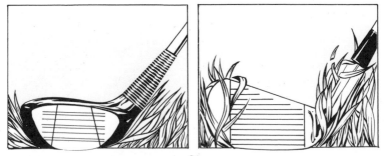

generally speaking, unless the ball is sitting up in the rough, leave the 3 wood in the bag. You would do better using a 4, 5 or 7 wood, and the worse the lie the more lofted the wood you should use. Strong men players do have an advantage over ladies when it comes to shots from the rough because regardless of how good your technique may be, the success rate from really bad lies will, to a large extent, depend on brute strength, so it is especially important for the ladies not to attempt shots beyond their physical capabilities. However, fairway woods come to the rescue as they glide through the rough rather than getting tangled in it(Fig 15.1).

The exit route

So having decided which club is the best to use, select the best line on which to play, which in many cases will not be directly towards the hole. You would be wise to avoid having to carry a bunker if the lie suggests that the ball might come out rather low (Fig 15.2). Likewise, if the lie is reasonably good, you must aim down rather than across the fairway so as not to land up in the rough on the other side.

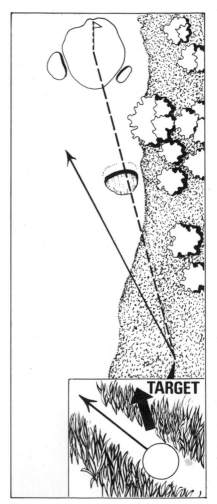

Fig 15.2. The ball will often come out low from rough, so avoid having to carry bunkers. You may also benefit from adjusting your aim if it allows you to swing the clubhead along a channel of shorter grass

Grass in the rough does not lie uniformly and very often you will see that the grass directly behind the ball is long and thick, whereas if you were to hit the ball in a slightly different direction, perhaps swinging along a line on which someone else had hit, you would stand a better chance of making good contact and good distance (Fig 15.2).

Remember that if it is not possible to reach the green, you want to play your next shot from the optimum position, which may mean hitting an easy 5 or 7 wood to lay up short of a bunker rather than trying to thrash your 4 wood and finishing in the bunker.

The set up and swing

Play the ball nearer the centre of your stance than usual, grip down the shaft a little and also grip more firmly. Keep your hands well ahead of the ball and put more weight on your left leg. Make the swing more upright so that the club does not catch the grass at the start of the backswing. Concentrate on swinging your *arms* up and down rather than making a good turn, and swing through the shot as much as possible, keeping your left hand

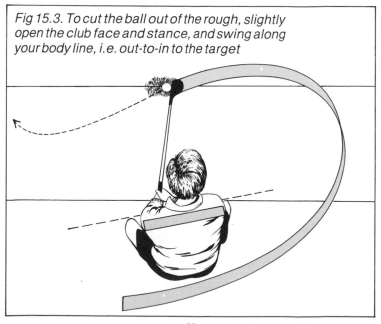

Fig 15.3. To cut the ball out of the rough, slightly open the club face and stance, and swing along your body line, i.e. out-to-in to the target

leading for as long as possible.

Another way to play these shots when the lie is not very good is to open the club face and aim yourself slightly left of your target, with the ball fairly central in your stance (Fig 15.3). This set up will enable you to make a steep backswing and cut across the ball. There will not be much left to right spin imparted because there will be too much grass between the club face and ball for clean contact. But the ball will come out on a line between the path of the swing and the direction of the club face. This resembles the fade shot with a wood described in Chapter 13.

If the lie is too bad for a wooden shot, you must accept this and take an iron. The only exception to the rule might be if you were only a yard or so into the rough and the fairway ahead had no hazards to concern you. The worst shot that you might hit with a wood would be a semi-topped shot, which would come out low and run. This shot is quite acceptable at the right time, expecially if the

Fig 15.4. For a short low running pitch from the rough, set up with your shoulders square, stance just open and the ball central. The hands are ahead of the ball at address and impact. The ball is punched out, with the back of the left wrist remaining firm

fairway ahead is downhill.

If you play an iron, you have decided to sacrifice distance for strategy, so do not ruin your wise decision by taking a long iron. Select a middle or short iron that you know you can definitely hit well. Play it in either manner described for the wood, but since the grass is likely to catch around the hosel, do have a firmer grip than normal.

For any shot in the rough you should have a practice swing in order to feel how the grass will affect the club. If the grass is lying towards you, the resistance is quite severe and you must be prepared for it — otherwise the club head will twist excessively. When the grass lies with the shot, the resistance is not so severe and the club head, especially with woods, will tend to glide through quite easily.

Any ball played from the rough will run more than a shot from the fairway, and this, at least, will help to make up for lost distance.

Short shots from the rough

Here I refer to shots of 100 yards and under where control and not distance is of greater importance. The type of lie will determine how accurate you can expect to be, since from a really bad lie even the best golfer in the world cannot be certain of what will happen.

The running pitch from short rough

A pitch shot from 70 to 80 yards where the ball is not lying too badly can be tackled in two ways, depending on whether or not height is essential. If there are no bunkers to carry then set up with your shoulders and hips parallel to the target, feet slightly open with your weight favouring the left foot. Keep the blade square with your hands well ahead of the ball, which should be central in your stance. Break your wrists early in the backswing and swing your arms up steeply. As you swing down keep your hands ahead of the club head and feel that you 'stab' the club head into the back of the ball (Fig 15.4). There is not much to follow through to the shot but the ball will come out quite readily, lower than a normal pitch, and run on landing. There is very much a 'hit and stop' feeling about this shot, with the hands taking most of the strain.

The high pitch from short rough

The difficulty of a pitch shot from 70 to 80 yards that has to carry a bunker depends on the lie of the ball. When it is sitting quite well with a nice cushion of grass beneath it, the shot presents no real problems. However, from a bad lie, the outcome is less certain and perhaps only the stronger and lower handicap player ought to attempt the shot.

To guarantee height, open the face of the appropriate club, then take your grip, keeping the left hand firmer than usual. Set up aiming slightly left, with the ball forward of centre in your stance but your weight evenly distributed. Keep your hands fairly level with, rather than too far ahead of, the ball so that you make full use of the club's loft. This type of address position creates an out-to-in swing, which helps to hit the ball on a higher trajectory (see Fig 14.4). The arms swing up steeply and the wrists break early in the backswing causing an upright action. As you swing back to the ball, feel that the right hand works *under* the left so that the blade remains open (Fig 15.5). Try to swing to a full finish with your hands high. Due to the fact that most of the force of the shot was designed to send the ball upwards, it will land softly and should not run too much. You must not be afraid to hit the ball quite hard, since the open stance and club face, hand action and thick grass will all reduce the distance of the shot. If you hit the ball too softly it will either remain in the rough or land in the bunker so do not try to be too clever — make certain that you get on the green. This shot requires rather more skill than the average higher handicap player might possess, and players in this category would be better advised to play a firmer wristed shot, starting with the hands ahead of the ball and the weight more on the left side. A slightly open stance and club face should provide adequate loft for the shot.

Thick rough

If the ball is lying in thick rough, the strength factor becomes more important, and so you must assess whether to carry a bunker will present too much of a problem. For men with a decent technique, the rough will not be as limiting as it is for women players, and particularly for the beginner. If reaching the green is out of the question, just play the ball back onto the fairway. The sand iron, with its heavy flange, is ideal for getting out of thick rough so do not be afraid to use it. Keep your weight and hands ahead of the ball, which is placed well back in an open stance opposite the right foot. Always have a practice swing as thick rough will want to severely twist the club head through the impact zone, and you must be prepared for this by gripping firmly. The upright arm swing, accompanied by an early wrist cock, will enable you to hit down on the ball. You will probably be unable to hit the ball but will strike the grass behind it, which will slow up the club head, reducing the power of the shot, so do not expect miracles from very bad lies.

Shots from around the green

Shots from the rough about 5 to 10 yards off the fringe, especially when the pin is not very far onto the green, can

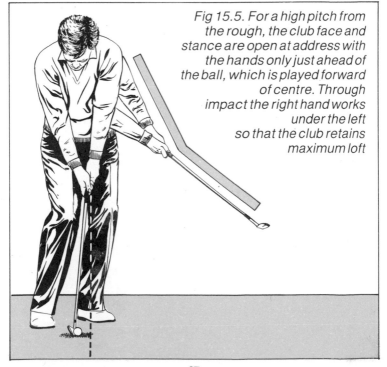

Fig 15.5. For a high pitch from the rough, the club face and stance are open at address with the hands only just ahead of the ball, which is played forward of centre. Through impact the right hand works under the left so that the club retains maximum loft

be difficult to judge. Unfortunately, sometimes the ball comes out 'hot', i.e. it flies off the club face and runs a lot on landing; at other times the grass behind the ball 'kills' the shot and the ball barely lands on the fringe. Consequently, you may be torn between being too firm with the shot or swinging too easy. The best club to use for the majority of these shots is the sand wedge, since its maximum loft and heavy flange will readily add height to the shot. Always grip down on the club, which allows you to be more positive without hitting the ball too far.

The passive handed shot

If the lie is not too bad, play the shot with passive hands. By this I mean that you must concentrate on swinging the club mainly with your arms, with no conscious strike with your hands. You thereby limit club head speed and can control the shot better. Having read this far in the chapter,

Fig 15.6. For a soft shot around the green from a reasonable lie in the rough, use an open set up and a passive handed action. Too much wrist cock in the backswing will give too much club head speed

I hope that by now you can imagine the set up needed — an open stance and club face with the body aimed just left of target, so that by swinging along the line of your body you will cut across the ball from out-to-in. Let your weight just favour the left foot, or keep it even on both feet if the lie is good. Position the ball centrally for reasonable lies, and slightly more forward for good lies. Although the club head needs to swing upwards away from the ball, swing your forearms up, keeping your wrists quiet (Fig 15.6). They will in fact break a little, but this should happen naturally rather than consciously. The whole swing should be very smooth, so take the club back far enough to keep the backswing and downswing almost at one pace. Do not be tempted to hit *at* the ball with your hands at the last minute, fearing that you do not have enough power for the shot. The back of the left hand should lead throughout so that both it and the club face finish facing more towards the sky than the ground. To maintain good rhythm, be sure to ease your knees towards the target at impact.

Having a mental image of playing the shot in slow motion helps create the correct feel for the shot. At first you will be tempted to hit the ball with your hands, but the feeling is very much one of dragging the club head *through* the ball with the forearms. By gripping a little firmer with both hands you will be able to keep your hands more passive. The more you play this shot, the more you will appreciate just how delicate you can afford to be with it. The main problem can be not having sufficient momentum in the swing, so that the club does not accelerate through the ball enough, and gets stuck in the grass. Good lies do not usually present this problem, but if the ball is sitting down slightly, make sure that you have enough force in the swing to keep swinging through the grass. By trying to make the length of the backswing and throughswing the same, you should then accelerate enough through the shot. The ball comes out quite softly and should not run too much on landing.

The very short chip

For very short shots, from, say, 2 or 3 yards off the green, use a sand wedge and set up as for the short pitch above, but grip well down on the club, even to the extent of having one or both hands on the shaft. For this delicate shot you just need to break the right wrist a little to make the backswing, and then be sure to hit through the ball, working the right hand *under* the left. Do not stab *at* the ball but keep the club head swinging through the grass, even with such a short swing, or you may leave the ball in the grass.

The grass 'bunker' shot

If the ball is lying badly around the green, you should consider playing the shot as though it were a bunker shot, i.e. aim to hit the grass perhaps an inch or two behind the ball rather than the ball itself. The shot is played using the same set up as for the passive handed pitch, with the ball positioned a little nearer the front foot. As you swing your arms up steeply, allow your wrists to break a little, and aim, and therefore look, at a spot in the grass behind the

Fig 15.7. When the lie is bad from just off the green, hit a 'bunker' shot where you aim to hit the grass about an inch behind the ball. To avoid catching the club head in the grass in the backswing, cock your wrists quite early

ball, concentrating on hitting it (Fig 15.7). You must hit right through the shot, keeping the back of the left hand looking towards the sky and swinging a little harder than you would do if you were hitting the ball itself. There is a little weight transference in the backswing but make sure that your legs move through the shot so that you finish with most of your weight on the left leg. At first you will find it hard to accept that you can hit the ball quite hard, even though you are so near to the hole. The grass that intervenes between the club head and ball cushions the force considerably, but you need to practise so that you can be confident that the extra power in the shot will land the ball on, and not over, the green.

Summary

I have tried to cover several options for escaping from the rough, but obviously you must decide for yourself which shot is not only the right one but the one that you feel happiest playing. I know many club golfers will play better long shots from the rough just by adopting my recommendations. Not too much practice is needed for these shots to improve — you just need to adapt to the situation. Do not try to be too clever around the green; remember that you are always better off *somewhere* on the green rather than off it. So let that always be the standard you bear in mind before deciding which shot to play.

CHAPTER SIXTEEN

Two-tier greens

Choosing the right shot at the right time in golf is half the battle of low scoring. All of us develop shots that we feel we can play without too much fear or the need for excessive concentration, and more often than not you are better off playing the shot you find easiest. However, on occasions you may have to opt for your least favourite shot to have any chance of getting the ball near the hole. In learning the correct aspects of the short game, the best maxim to adopt is to putt the ball if possible. However, if it is not possible, then chip it and leave the pitch shot as the last option. This advice is based on the fact that usually a bad putt will give a better result than a bad chip, and a bad chip will give a better result than a bad pitch. Always consider both the lie of the ball, the intervening ground and the pin position before making a decision how to play the shot. This, of course, holds true for the short game department but in this chapter I want to cover in some detail how best to play shots that involve two-tier greens.

Putting to a two-tier green

For the first example, let us assume that you are just off the green on the closely mown fringe, which is fairly smooth and even with the hole cut in the middle of the top tier. In this situation you would be best advised to putt the ball since it is the easiest shot to play (Fig 16.1).

Most two-tier greens are fairly deep and it is more than likely that you will have a very long putt, which needs striking quite firmly. To assist in this, stand a little taller and grip nearer the end of your putter than usual. You may need to add a little extra wrist break to your putting action in order to get enough speed into the shot. So in the backswing allow your right wrist to hinge a little, but be sure to keep the back of the left wrist firm at impact and beyond. With more action from the right hand it is easy to drag or pull the putt left, so try to keep the putter head moving towards the target at least 18 inches after impact. Pace will be difficult to judge and obviously will depend on the total length of the putt as well as the

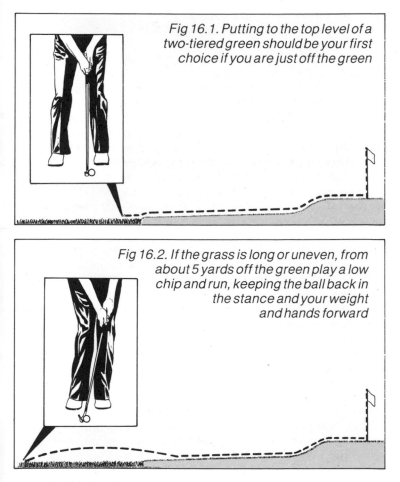

Fig 16.1. Putting to the top level of a two-tiered green should be your first choice if you are just off the green

Fig 16.2. If the grass is long or uneven, from about 5 yards off the green play a low chip and run, keeping the ball back in the stance and your weight and hands forward

severity of the slope between you and the hole. Naturally the slope will slow the ball so do not be afraid to strike the putt firmly. I am sure that you would be better off 5 feet past the hole rather than 'babying' the shot only to see the ball roll back down the slope and be faced with the same shot again. So strike the ball crisply, trying to keep the putter head accelerating towards the hole. If you are not putting straight up the slope but across it, remember that the ball will break in the direction of the lower level of the green. One tip to help you judge the pace of the putt is to imagine that the slope does not exist and that the putt is on a flat green with the hole further away. So, for instance, you could imagine that a 16 yard putt up the slope is perhaps an 18 yard putt on a flat surface.

Chipping to a two-tiered green

When the ball is further off the green, perhaps 3 or
4 yards, and the grass is not smooth enough to allow you
to putt, and the hole is on the top tier, then you should
chip and run the ball. Using a less lofted club, perhaps a 5,
6 or 7 iron, depending on your preference, set more
weight on your left leg and play the ball back of centre of
a narrow, open stance (Fig 16.2). Keep your hands ahead
of the ball opposite your left thigh, which means that the
7 iron will become hooded, making it more like a 6 iron.
This set up makes it easy for you to hit the ball on a slight
descending arc. Of course it is impossible for me to tell
you how hard you should hit the ball as this will depend
not only on the depth and speed of the green but also on
the steepness of the slope. These are factors that you
must consider while assessing the shot and taking a
couple of practice swings. However, the same principle
applies as with the putt — that you are better off on the
top level but past the hole rather than on the lower level of
the green. As with putting, you may find it helpful to
imagine that the green is flat but that the pin is further
away. The stroke should be firm-wristed and smooth. Try
to make the backswing and throughswing the same
length, and you will then produce a more rhythmical
stroke rather than a stabbing action. On the throughswing
allow the right knee to ease towards the target, which will
enable you to keep the back of the left wrist firm and
moving towards the target. The ball will land on the lower
level, then run up the slope to the top tier. These shots
need practice for although the technique is simple, judging
the distance accurately is essential for success.

To pitch or chip and run?

Imagine that the ball is 70 yards from the hole, which is
cut on the top tier. How you choose to play this shot will
depend greatly on how good a player you are. Certainly
the higher handicap player would be better off trying to
land the ball on the lower tier and letting it run up the
slope (Fig 16.3) whereas the better player might well be
able to judge pitching it onto the top tier provided that the
circumstances are right (Fig 16.4).
   To play the lower running shot, you should select

perhaps anything from a 9 to a 7 iron depending on how you see the shot and how fast the ground is running. Ideally you still want to land the ball on the front on the green since you are less likely to get an awkward bounce. If the fairway is close cut and flat, then you could safely land the ball there and your choice of club will be influenced by this factor. Set up with a fairly narrow open stance, but with your shoulders parallel to the ball to target line. With your weight favouring your left side, perhaps 60:40, play the ball in the centre, or just back of centre, in your stance and position your hands ahead of the ball. The swing should be made mainly with your arms, keeping your hands fairly passive and firm and ahead of the ball at impact. There is no need to swing your arms up steeply in the backswing; instead, just swing them back quite naturally so that the clubhead makes more of a 'U' than a 'V' shaped arc. The throughswing will be abbreviated somewhat so that the whole action feels more like a punch shot. The length and power of your

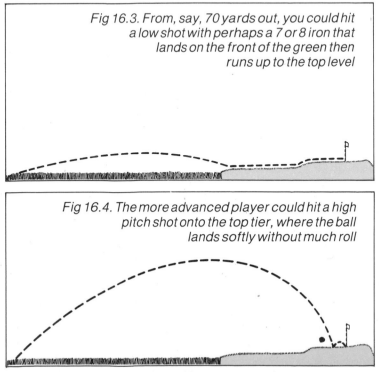

Fig 16.3. From, say, 70 yards out, you could hit a low shot with perhaps a 7 or 8 iron that lands on the front of the green then runs up to the top level

Fig 16.4. The more advanced player could hit a high pitch shot onto the top tier, where the ball lands softly without much roll

swing will be governed by the length of the shot and choice of club. It would therefore be a very valuable exercise to hit balls varying distances of, say, between 50 and 100 yards with different clubs. Naturally it would be best if you could carry out this practice onto a two-tiered green as you would then be able to see how the ball reacts on landing. However, if this is not possible, simply practise hitting to a target, e.g. an umbrella, and you will learn to judge how hard to hit a 9 iron 50 yards, or a 7 iron 80 yards. How far the ball runs on landing will come with experience, and also will vary according to the conditions.

Remember that a less lofted club, such as a 6 or 7 iron, will fly lower and run more on landing than a more lofted club such as a 9 iron. Once you can judge how hard to hit the ball so that it lands on or near the front of the green even if the strength of the shot is slightly misjudged, you will be able to build on your experience. If there are no serious hazards over the back of the green such as out of bounds, a deep bunker or very thick rough, you may be better erring on the side of hitting the ball too hard rather than too soft. Often a two-tier green is banked at the back so that any shot hit too hard will be prevented from going too far, or may even roll back down off the bank onto the green. Take all these points into consideration before playing the shot and you may find that being slightly more attacking will result in a much improved shot.

If you are a lower handicap player, then you may prefer to pitch the ball onto the top tier. This shot requires more precise judgement of distance than the lower running shot, but if you know how far you hit your sand iron, wedge or 9 iron, and are good at judging the depth of a shot, then you might well get better results from pitching the ball all the way. However, before deciding to play this shot, I would recommend that you consider the following points carefully:

1 The ball needs to be lying well — if it is in the rough, it will run on landing and you may not be able to stop it on the green.
2 If it is on a bare lie, you will probably not be able to use your sand iron as the flange will tend to bounce off the ground and you risk thinning the shot.
3 If the green is very hard, and especially if the top tier is quite shallow, you will find it difficult to stop the ball on the green.

4 If you misjudge the shot and hit the ball beyond the green, you may be in a worse position than being on the lower tier.

So ideally to pitch to the top tier, you need it to be sufficiently deep, the green to be yielding, and to have a decent lie. Whilst backspin will help to stop the ball, if the shot is not very long, say, less than a full sand iron, you will not be able to hit the ball hard enough to get maximum backspin and must therefore use elevation as well to stop the ball. To ensure this, address the ball with your weight 60:40 in favour of your left side, a slightly open stance and shoulder line, and the club face open a little. This set up will create an out-to-in swing path which adds height to the shot. Swing your arms up in the backswing allowing your wrists to break naturally. As you swing down make certain that your knees ease towards the target as you strike the ball. Keep the left arm and hand in charge, but do not become too wristy on the shot — your set up should guarantee enough height.

However, if you are lucky enough to find a very good lie where the ball is sitting on a cushion of grass, set your weight more evenly or slightly in favour of the right leg at address, and this will increase the height of the shot.

It is absolutely essential that you hit the ball far enough; the height of the shot means that it is most unlikely to roll up the slope. You should practise using the short irons until you become adept not only at hitting the ball the required distance but also at judging the distance on the course. The fact that all pins are not the same height can lead you to misjudge the depth. It is often helpful to walk half-way to the hole, then pace back to your ball. By doubling the number of paces you will have a good idea of the length of the shot. Of course, this presupposes that you already know how far you hit each club, and also that you do not hold up play.

Whichever shot you choose to play to a two-tiered green, you must be 100 per cent certain and confident when you stand over the ball that you are playing the right shot. Indecision will undoubtedly lead to a poor result.

CHAPTER SEVENTEEN

Banked and elevated greens

If you just miss a banked or elevated green, you will be faced with a shot that can be played in several ways. Which shot you choose must be decided not only by your standard of play and which shots you are most capable of executing well, but also by how the ball lies and how much green you have to work with.

Let us assume that you have hit the ball 5 to 10 yards wide of the green and that the hole is in the middle of the green, which is about 2 to 3 feet above you. If the ball is sitting reasonably well, your first option should be to putt the ball, provided that the ground is not too uneven nor the grass too long (Fig 17.1). This would be almost like putting to the top level of a two-tier green (see Chapter 16). If the ball is sitting badly or the ground and the grass are too uneven, then chip the ball. Set up with the ball back of centre in an open stance, your weight more on the left side, your shoulders parallel to the target line and hands well ahead of the ball. From this set up just remember to hit down slightly on the ball and you will strike it correctly. Make the swing using your forearms rather than your hands.

You would also use this set up and shot if you had missed the green by more than 10 yards when to putt may be impossible but you still want to run the ball rather than pitch it (Fig 17.2). You must make allowances for the roughness of the ground between you and the pin when deciding how hard to hit the ball. I would recommend an 8 or 7 iron for this shot to give you enough forward roll and elevation.

In each of these instances, even the lower handicap player should consider playing a running shot rather than always trying to pitch the ball. Whatever standard of player you may be, the shot that is the easier and has the greater degree of tolerance of a mis-strike is the best choice.

When faced with a shot from just beside an elevated green, which is perhaps 5 to 10 feet above you, you might be able to play either of the two shots just mentioned. If the grass on the bank is cut quite short you could chip or putt the ball but you will have to hit it quite hard. Whilst the outcome from these shots may be less than perfect, if you are a high handicap player, then getting the ball onto

*Fig 17.1. If the ground
and grass are not too
uneven, your first option
should be to putt
to an elevated green*

*Fig 17.2. From further
away from the green,
play a low chip
and run shot
using perhaps a 7 iron*

the green, even if it is not too near the pin, is your
principal aim.

If you are a low handicap golfer you should consider
two other options. You could choose to punch the ball
into the bank, which tends to stun the ball, making it jump
up in the air and then run onto the green (Fig 17.3). This is
often a good shot to play if the hole is cut near to your
side of the green. However, it does need practice since
you will have to hit the ball fairly firmly into the bank, and
should you misjudge the shot it might prove costly. Set up
as for the chip and run shot already described in this
chapter and, using a medium iron, punch the ball into the
bank, about half-way up. This will kill most of the power in
the shot and the ball should then roll onto the green with
little force. The nearer you are to the bank, the easier the
shot. If you have missed an elevated green by, say, 10 to

15 yards and the pin is cut close to your side of the green, this shot could still be considered, but judging the power and elevation so that the ball hits the bank at the desired spot becomes more difficult.

The other option you have is to pitch the ball onto the green (Fig 17.4). This is the more difficult shot to play, often requiring a delicate touch, which can lead to quitting on the shot if you are not careful. You also need a reasonable lie where the ball is neither sitting on bare ground nor nestled down in thick rough. You should use your most lofted club, i.e. the sand iron, and set up slightly open with your stance and shoulder line, ball forward of centre and with the club face just open.

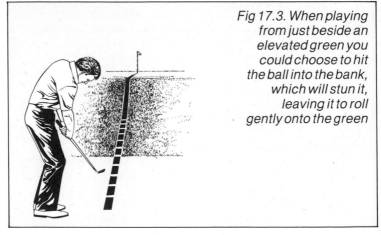

Fig 17.3. When playing from just beside an elevated green you could choose to hit the ball into the bank, which will stun it, leaving it to roll gently onto the green

Fig 17.4. If you pitch to an elevated green, open the stance and club face, then swing through the shot, feeling that you are dragging the club head back into the ball. Keep the back of the left hand facing skywards after impact and the ball will fly high and land softly